RUNAWAY AFRICAN

How It Started

Kene Louis

TABLE OF CONTENT

INTRODUCTION

Run for Greener Pastures

The movement of Nigerians looking for greener fields abroad is no news except for the rate at which they are leaving represents a reason to worry, as they assume an essential part in the development and improvement of an economy.

Africa's greatest economy is honoured with an enormous, energetic, and youthful populace which includes more than 65% of its populace. Be that as it may, unfortunately, the monetary difficulties in the nation have neglected to foster them intellectually and financially, compelling them to move to different nations for greener fields.

As indicated by a new overview by the World Bank, 50% of Nigerian young people need to leave the country. The nation set third in West Africa among the countries surveyed, following just Liberia (70%) and Sierra Leone (60%).

In like manner as far as visas given to the UK, Nigeria recorded a rise of 234.7 per cent to 18,580 in the initial nine months of 2021 from 5,551 in a similar time of 2019.

CHAPTER 1

Risk It All

The frenzy for a superior life in America and Europe by Nigerian and African young people is starting to seem to be a self-destruction mission, where one is very nearly 100% of a dead end, yet unequipped for beating a retreat. Pictures exuding from doomed excursions, and, surprisingly, shameful stories from fortunate survivors have neglected to prevent those that are never going to budge from taking a stab. Call it trust or sadness, it seems now is the right time to apply local answers to stop sporadic movement and deal with individuals as customary cures seem unequipped for stemming the tide.

Indian first Prime Minister and a focal figure in the country's governmental issues when freedom, Jawaharlal Nehru it was who said, "Evil unrestrained develops, malicious endured harms the entire framework."

This gives off an impression of what is going on that Nigeria has wound up with the uncontrolled unlawful movement and dealing of capable young people to different regions of the planet, particularly Europe, apparently looking for greener fields because of difficulty in the nation brought about by degenerate lawmakers.

Week-in, week-out, neighbourhood and worldwide media are flooded with stories and pictures of collections of Nigerians and Africans washed shorewards by the tide in the Mediterranean Sea. Yet, so impenetrable are those that are keen on taking a stab at the voice of reason that even the ghostly possibility of them winding up in the guts of the sea makes next to no difference to them. All they are keen on is leaving on the long, dangerous and difficult excursion through the desert to Libya, and eventually Europe.

While the outing endures, most travellers, particularly females are physically disregarded, hoodwinked or dealt with even as their protected appearance in Europe is without authorization to live or work.

Coming to Libya is only one piece of the intricate two-section trip. Regardless, a few unfortunate ones among them frequently get deported from Libya, where they ordinarily visit before setting out on the last leg of the trip to Europe.

Youthful Nigerians make up the biggest populace of the developing progression of travellers from Africa to created nations. In 2016, more than 20,000 associated with the Mediterranean Sea crossing were accounted to be from Nigeria.

Also, from 2017 until late 2019, many Nigerian travellers were deported from different destinations including Italy, Libya and South Africa. These young
people embark on very risky journeys across the globe, and casualties continue to increase daily.

Understanding their explanations behind leaving the nation is significant assuming Nigeria will stem the tide.

A review was led to lay out the degree to which youngsters matured somewhere in the range of 15 and 35 were vulnerable to unlawful relocation and whether they knew about what is involved. Additionally,an analysis of the mentalities and methods for surviving embraced by unpredictable travellers getting back to Nigeria was conducted.

I zeroed in on three gatherings of migrants who fall into the "irregular migration" classification. The first was the people who showed up in a nation illicitly. The second, the individuals who showed up legitimately - for example, given vacationer or understudy visas - and afterwards exceeded the period covered by their visas. Lastly, refuge searchers whose cases have been dismissed and who have not left the country as required.

My discoveries showed that most youngsters who moved under unpredictable conditions were roused by three variables: monetary reasons, terrible governance and social media.

Most said they accepted that the "end will without a doubt legitimize the means". What's more, they saw the capacity to travel abroad as an indication of progress.

Research

We led interviews with 63 youngsters who had not yet left the country in four Nigerian urban communities: Lagos, Ibadan, Ile-Ife and Benin City. We designated those powerless to movement. These incorporated the jobless people, in their last year at a tertiary-level training organization and those who took part in

Nigeria's obligatory National Youth Service Corps. We additionally included seven youngsters who had attempted to relocate yet had been returned.

We additionally ran separate centres gathering conversations for people. We picked individuals in light of whether they knew about the course of unpredictable relocation.

Once in the gatherings, we posed inquiries to decide their knowledge of the idea of sporadic relocation. Most said they were. We likewise settled that most were new to formal migration strategies and that the greater part didn't have a substantial visa.

Most knew somebody by and by who had gone out of the country through unlawful means like producing a visa, utilizing unapproved specialists, and heading out to "Europe by street" - as sporadic movement is alluded to in the famous maxim.

Most communicated uplifting outlooks about sporadic relocation, expressing that the end would legitimize the means. They generally shared the view that travellers were far superior to the individuals who remained behind since they approached a superior personal satisfaction.

Bola, a 29-year-old female jobless youth from Osun State, declared:

Genuinely, the people who relocate outside the nation frequently live much better than we in Nigeria. They partake in a steady power supply, and great climate, eat a decent eating regimen and to a sensible degree, they are.

Early this year, 25-year-old printing machine repairer Abraham Osahon, trusted in a companion that he was migrating to Norway, through Libya, having been fed up with how he was living in Edo State.

Before deciding to migrate, Osahon, who had a vehicle and was living in a one-room condo, his cousin said, was persuaded that life out there was superior to the daily routine he was experiencing. He was likewise brimming with laments that those he supported abroad, and a portion of his companions, who left prior had overlooked him.

Bloody reports getting out and about day to day, in any case, Osahon decided to go by street through Libya, and, surprisingly, paid more than the base expense for a better degree of solace while crossing the desert. He was fortunate to come to Italy in under two months, where he is presently getting prepared as a transporter.

Another 18-year-old fortunate migrant, Joy, like Osahon, has been intrigued with travelling abroad for quite a while. Along the line, an "aunt" went along and elected to bankroll her trip to Italy. Likewise in no less than one month, she was in Italy, from where she let The Guardian know that on appearance in that nation, she and others were first placed in a camp before things were figured out.

On her central goal in Italy, she brazenly said, "ordinary level" which alludes to prostitution.

"It took me one month to get to Italy, yet we were fortunate we gone through a territory not routinely watched by security offices, and we were around 200 in the boat. I have begun "work," however I do as such during the day due to the cold around evening time. Here, I pay for my convenience and pay my aunt for the cash she spent to bring me here."

She, in any case, would not uncover the amount she would reimburse altogether before she recaptures her opportunity as she affirmed she was under oath and not to unveil that to anyone.

The Drivers

The sporadic movement will in general rot notwithstanding monetary misfortune. Nigeria's economy is not doing so well. Unemployment among youths is especially high at 36.50% in 2018.

What's more, poverty levels have deteriorated. In 2019, the quantity of very unfortunate Nigerians was assessed at 91.6 million, almost 50% of the nation's complete populace. Nigeria additionally has 87 million individuals living in poverty.

This increment is one reason Nigerians leave the nation looking for Greener Pastures. All in all to track down security, work and better approaches for life in different nations.

A new report on sporadic relocation optimized these discoveries. In reporting the encounters of Africans who had relocated to Europe utilizing sporadic means, it distinguishes an absence of chance to apply effect on their legislatures concerning movement.

More or less, the following are five motivations behind why most Nigerian young people are leaving the country:

1. Poverty

2. Unemployment

3. Insecurity/Uncertainty

4. Poor Education

5. Corruption

CHAPTER2

Insecurity

The issue of insecurity in Nigeria has become something of a grave worry to all benevolent residents the greater part of who keep on considering how the nation showed up in such an obnoxious circumstance where nobody is protected; more regrettable still, as opposed to subside, the issue is raising and presently thoroughly crazy. First and foremost, let us think about the significance of the word: instability. As indicated by the high-level students' word reference, instability just means a condition of not being protected or secured. From a more extensive or more extensive viewpoint, uncertainty surmises a condition of an overall breakdown of the rule of law or a circumstance where the residents of a nation are presented with a wild peril by which everybody lives in anxiety toward anything that could happen the following second. Uncertainty, in this way, proposes what is going on where a condition of turmoil is released on an overall people and human existence becomes 'terrible, brutish and short to get the language of Thomas Hobbes. Uncertainty in Nigeria is certainly not another peculiarity.

The nation has consistently confronted different troublesome difficulties at various times. As soon as the 1960s, the nation was engaged in a three-year Nationwide conflict that obliterated specific pieces of the country. Such countless honest individuals lost their lives to a conflict they neither expected nor upheld. All through the period the conflict endured, there was such a lot of frailty in the nation prompting the deficiency of countless lives. Soon after the conflict, one more type of weakness was released on the nation by outfitted burglars. At a time, it got so uncontrolled and unnerving that the tactical government at the time declared a declaration suggesting a terminating crew for furnished looters. It was at that period that rough outfitted burglars like Ishola Oyenusi and his group were executed at the bar ocean side. From that point forward, the country has seen various gatherings of outfitted criminals threatening the whole scene, for example, Lawrence Anini and Shina Rambo, and it has brought about the development of an alternate crew of the police force burdened with the obligation of keeping men of the hidden world under control.

As of late, herders have turned into one more wellspring of frailty in Nigeria. Numerous guiltless ranchers are being killed on the homesteads they have carried on with on their whole resides by herders a significant number of who currently bear modern weapons. The pattern has prompted a lot of irritation between the Fulani and the greater part of their host networks. It has likewise caused the refusal by a large portion of the southern provincial networks to acknowledge various ideas by the public authority for settling the herders.

The friction between the National Government and most southern leaders has arrived at a top as most southern governors have begun passing the counter-open brushing regulations which would refuse the herders from moving openly across individuals' homesteads. In any case, as the conflict seethes on, many lives are being lost and the pertinence of the public authority is being called to address.

Strict radicalism is likewise a major area of strength for militating against harmony in the territory of uncertainty that Nigeria has unexpectedly become. For over a decade, the North Eastern, North Western and without a doubt, most pieces of the North have been desolated by fanatical zealots known as Boko Haram. A few a great many individuals have been killed while a huge segment of individuals was uprooted and presently live in Inside Dislodged camps spread across the entire northern states. Furthermore, hijacking for recovery has since entered Nigeria's dictionary and the issue is turning out to be exceptionally recalcitrant. Blameless younger students particularly in the North are being hijacked every day taken into the profound woodland while their folks are tossed into extraordinary hopelessness. From the previous, consequently, there is no denying that frailty in Nigeria today is more articulated than in the bygone eras, and it is reminiscent of the way that the public authority has an extraordinary errand before it to convey whatever is expected to reestablish harmony and predictability to the land. It ought not to be awkward for Nigeria to look for unfamiliar help assuming need be. Each administration must guarantee the security of the lives and properties of the residents and anything way is taken on to ensure harmony and quietness isn't just gladly received yet additionally attractive.

There are worldwide worries over the pattern of uncertainty in a few countries, all the more so when it includes foes of the state that carry weapons and release commotion on honest residents.

There has been a cooperative methodology among various nations and establishments to handling weakness, particularly psychological oppression, the most difficult worldwide security issue. There are serious areas of strength among security and monetary development since organizations and speculations can't endeavour in a perilous climate. Nigeria has had its portion of frailty throughout recent many years. As per the Global Terrorism Index (GTI), Nigeria has two of the five deadliest terror groups in the world, in particular; Boko Haram and Fulani fanatics. Nigeria was evaluated as the third most awful country with uncertainty on the planet in 2020 by the Global Terrorism Index (GTI), behind Afghanistan and Iraq. These appraisals have been of huge worry to security experts and the government.

Notwithstanding the public authority's huge financing in safeguard, line security, a cooperative exertion with other adjoining countries, changes in security structures, contrition of many fear mongers, and the interior emergency between Boko Haram and Islamic State West African Province (ISWAP) over matchless quality, and enduring arrangement is as yet a worry for specialists and the public authority.

Late security assaults in various pieces of Nigeria, particularly the seizure of younger students in the North-West, North-Focal, and North-East, have expanded the quantity of out-of-younger students. This has north of 10 million youngsters out of school, the most noteworthy on the planet as indicated by the United Nations International Children's Emergency Fund (UNICEF). These figures were projected to demolish by the World Bank in 2022. As per the World Bank, Nigeria has been the world's poverty capital starting around 2016. This has been credited to the difficulties of uncertainty in Nigeria, where individuals' huge wellsprings of financial vocation have altogether been impacted by psychological warfare, banditry, and farmers/herders' regular conflicts. The failure of ranchers to have a good sense of reassurance going to their homesteads and the backwoods being involved by criminal components have additionally impacted food security and food costs in Nigeria.

Insecurity in Nigeria has disturbed the production network as road transport that is consistently used to move labour and products from the North toward the Southern part has been demolished over the apprehension about capturing and redirecting merchandise. The Nigerian business climate has been worried about venture wellbeing in Nigeria as a few unfamiliar financial backers are relocating to other more secure adjoining nations for speculation. The potential in

the travel industry has similarly been impacted by
security worries for tourists.

CHAPTER 3

Poor Education

One in each five of the world's out-of-younger students is in Nigeria.

Although essential training is authoritatively free and mandatory, around 10.5 million of the country's kids matured 5-14 years are not in school.

As assumed, the schooling area ought to be given bunches of consideration since it gives space for the nation's turn of events. Sadly, the quality and standard of schooling in Nigeria are poor since it has not been given sufficient consideration.

Nigeria runs an organization framework, so the Nigerian schooling system is regulated by the Service of Training. The school system at the government level is overseen by the Service of Instruction. This incorporates the administration of government colleges and schools. The state government-funded schools and tertiary establishments are controlled provincially by the Service at the state level.

The explanations behind poor education in Nigeria are as follows:

1. Poor Financing

The first and conceivably quite possibly of the best test confronting schooling in Nigeria is lacking subsidizing by the bureaucratic, state and nearby legislatures. In the year 2017, Nigeria's schooling area was again distributed a lot lower than the 26% of the public spending plan suggested by the Unified Countries.

The worldwide association prescribed the monetary benchmark to empower countries satisfactorily cook for rising instruction requests. Yet, in the proposition introduced to the Public Gathering, President Muhammadu Buhari designated just 7.04% of the 8.6 trillion 2018 financial plan for schooling.

The complete aggregate apportioned to the area is N605.8 billion, with N435.1 billion for intermittent use, N61.73 billion for capital use and N109.06 billion for the Widespread Fundamental Instruction Commission.

2. Poor Administration

Poor administration and blunder have disabled most areas in the country not abandoning the schooling area. The public authority's demeanour towards significant issues of instruction, particularly its quality, is lazy.

Legislatures at all levels are more worried about issues that are not as significant as instruction and this may be devastating the area.

3. Corruption

Debasement is one of the serious issues in the nation and the instructive area isn't a special case. There are accounts of teachers gathering pay-offs from understudies in return for good grades, college directors requesting cash from understudies to have their test results assembled and submitted to the (required) Public Youth Administration Corps, and confirmation searchers paying cash to get entrance into colleges, etc.

Likewise, school reserves implied for compensations, upkeep, etc are being redirected for individual use and botched. This cuts across every one of the levels of the area; colleges, private and public auxiliary schools.

4. Absence of Responsibilityand Control

This is an issue influencing Nigeria as well as most nations on who precisely controls the instructive area. Is it bureaucratic, state or neighbourhood government, for instance, the control of essential training is neither completely in the hand of the central government, nor state or nearby government, this is an extraordinary hindrance to successful instructive improvement at the fundamental level.

Works that should have been done are being passed around and no level of government needs to assume any liability.

5. Absence of Infrastructure

In previous years, schools and other professional organizations have fallen because of wretched disregard by governments. Our tertiary foundations need to fall into incapacitation and the results of such schools are not given satisfactory preparation to contend with different results of another country.

Many schools miss the mark on hardware for favourable learning, most particularly for science down-to-earth classes, and those that case to have are dealing with the old ones. Subsequently, the understudies just get familiar with the hypothetical advances instead of doing the reasonable angle. Additionally, the libraries in schools are deficient in the required books, diaries and magazines.

6. Indiscipline

Indiscipline is so endemic in the area that we know about faction killings pretty much consistently in the media, understudies are not generally worried about scholastic greatness.

7. Absence of Teaching Aids

Showing helps or gadgets utilized by an instructor to upgrade or breathe life into study hall guidance. There is an extensive variety of shows which can be sound, video, books, DVDs, Projectors, PCs and so on which are not accommodated educators in this manner making education troublesome.

8. Shaky Educational plan and Subject

A successful educational plan gives teachers, students, and administrators a quantifiable arrangement and construction for conveying quality schooling. It goes about as a guide for teachers and students to follow the way to scholastic achievement.

CHAPTER 4

Corruption

Corruption in Nigeria is a steady peculiarity. In 2012, Nigeria was assessed to have lost more than $400 billion to corruption since its freedom. In 2021, the nation positioned 154th in the 180 nations recorded in Transparency International's Corruption Index (with South Sudan, at 180th, being the worst)

Nigerian legislators end up in serious areas of strength for influence and abundance because of their associations with the oil and gas ventures in Nigeria. These gas businesses are heavily influenced by the state-possessed Nigerian National Petroleum Company (NNPC). Oil and gas exports account for more than 90% of all Nigerian export revenues. While numerous lawmakers own or have shares in these ventures, tax revenue from the energy area is lessened and the advantages of Nigeria's energy abundance are not uniformly disseminated all through the country with Lagos State benefitting disproportionately. Oil and gas incomes, consequently, represent by far most of the bureaucratic financial plan and the compensations of government authorities.

Vote fixing by ideological groups in races is far and wide and corruption is endemic inside government. Business game plans and family loyalties overwhelm legislative arrangements preparing for lawmakers, authorities and their business partners who together make up the decision first class to guarantee that they generally become affluent through the background arrangements and the granting of productive agreements to leaned lean allies. In 2018 numerous administration representatives got yearly compensations above $1 million. Debasement goes through each level of the Nigerian government. From significant agreement extortion at the top, through frivolous pay-off plans, misappropriation and holding onto compensations from fake workers, it is assessed that corruption inside the state contraption costs the country billions of dollars annually.

A. History and Cases (How Corruption Began)

The ascent of policy implementation and the disclosure of oil and petroleum gas are two significant occasions accepted to have prompted the supported expansion in the occurrence of degenerate practices in the country.

Endeavours have been made by the public authority to limit corruption through the establishment of regulations and the requirement of uprightness frameworks however with little achievement.

Insatiability, garish way of life, customs, and individuals' perspectives is accepted to have prompted corruption. Another main driver is tribalism. Companions and families looking for favour from authorities can force burdens on the moral attitude of the authority as these families view government authorities as holding roads for their survival and gain.

1. Pre-Independence and the First Republic

Corruption, however common, was kept at sensible levels during the First Republic. Nonetheless, the instances of corruption during the period were at times blurred by political infighting. Azikiwe was the main major political figure explored for sketchy practices. In

1944, a firm having a place with Azikiwe and his family purchased a bank in Lagos. The bank was secured to fortify nearby control of the monetary business. Yet, a report about exchanges done by the bank showed that Azikiwe had surrendered as an executive of the bank, the ongoing director was a specialist of his. The report composed that the vast majority of the settled-up capital of the African Mainland Bank was from the Eastern Local Monetary Partnership.

In western Nigeria, politician Adegoke Adelabu was examined following charges of political defilement evened out against him by the resistance.

In the Northern district, against the scenery of debasement charges evened out against some local power authorities in Borno. The Northern Government established the Standard Presents request to thwart any further break of guidelines. Later on, it was the English organization that was blamed for degenerate practices in the consequences of decisions which enthroned a Fulani political initiative in Kano, reports later connecting the English specialists to constituent inconsistencies were found.

2. Gowon Administration (August 1966 - July 1975)

Debasement for a large portion of Yakubu Gowon's organization was avoided general visibility until 1975. Be that as it may, informed authorities voiced their interests. Pundits said Gowon's lead representatives behaved like masters regulating their inclinations. He was seen as meek and confronted with degenerate components in his administration.

In 1975, a defilement outrage encompassing the importation of concrete overwhelmed numerous authorities of the guard service and the national bank of Nigeria. Authorities were subsequently blamed for distorting transport pronouncements and blowing up how much concrete was to be bought.

During the Gowon organization, two people from the central belt of the nation were blamed for debasement. The Nigerian government controlled the papers, so the Everyday Times and the New Nigerian gave extraordinary exposure to censures of the organization of Gomwalk, and Bureaucratic Chief Joseph Tarka by the two pundits. A circumstance that might flag a reason for critical activity against corruption.

3. Murtala Administration (1975 - February 1976)

In 1975, the organization of Murtala Mohammed rolled out reformist improvements. After a tactical upset carried it to control, the new government terminated countless earlier government authorities and government employees, a considerable lot of whom had been condemned for the abuse of force they used under the to a great extent uninformed military of Gowon.

4. Obasanjo Administration (February 1976 - September 1979)

The main organization of Olusegun Obasanjo was a continuation of the Murtala Mohammed organization and was centred on finishing the progress program to a majority rules government, as well as executing the public improvement plans. Significant activities including building new treatment facilities, and pipelines, growing the public transportation and carriers as well as facilitating FESTAC were finished during this organization. Some of these public activities were courses to circulate leans toward and advance associated lawmakers. The renowned Afrobeat performer, Fela Kuti, sang differently about significant outrages including the global telecom firm ITT drove by Boss MKO Abiola in

Nigeria, which the then head of state, Gen Olusegun Obasanjo, was related with. Likewise, the Activity Feed the Country Program and the related land gets under the Land Use Pronouncement carried out by the then head of state were utilized as conductors to remunerate comrades, and his now-renowned Otta Farm Nigeria (OFN) was probably a task borne out of this embarrassment.

5. Shagari Administration (October 1979 - December 1983)

Defilement was considered unavoidable during the organization of Shehu Shagari.A couple of government structures bafflingly burst into flames after examiners began to test the funds of the authorities working in the buildings. In late 1985, examinations concerning the breakdown of the dead Johnson Mathey Bank of London shed light on a portion of the maltreatments carried on during the subsequent republic. The bank went about as a channel to move hard cash for some party individuals in Nigeria. A couple of driving authorities and lawmakers had amassed a lot of cash. They tried to move the cash out of the country with the assistance of Asian merchants by giving import licenses.

In 1981, a rice deficiency prompted allegations of debasement against the NPN government. Deficiencies and ensuing charges were accelerated by protectionism. After its political race, the Nigerian government chose to safeguard neighbourhood rice ranchers from imported items. A permitting framework was made to restrict rice imports. In any case, allegations of partiality and government-upheld theory were evened out against numerous authorities.

6. Buhari Administration (December 1983 - August 1985)

In 1985, a cross-segment of lawmakers was sentenced for degenerate practices under the public authority of General Muhammadu Buhari, however, the actual organization was just engaged with a couple of occasions of passing moral judgment. Some refer to the bags' embarrassment which additionally unintentionally elaborates then customs leader Atiku Abubakar, who later became VP in 1999, and was arraigned for different demonstrations of defilement. "The 53 bags adventure emerged in 1984 during the money change work-out arranged by the Buhari junta when it requested that each case showing up in the nation ought to be assessed regardless of the situation with the individual behind such. The 53 bags were, nonetheless, carried through the Murtala Muhammed Air terminal without check by warriors purportedly at the command of Major Mustapha Jokolo, the then confidant to Gen. Buhari. Atiku was around then the Region Controller of Customs accountable for the Murtala Muhammed Airport."

7. Babangida Administration (August 1985 - August 1993)

The system of General Ibrahim Babangida or IBB has been viewed as the body that sanctioned defilement. His organization wouldn't give a record of the Bay Conflict bonus, which has been assessed to be $12.4 billion. He manipulated the main fruitful political decision throughout the entire existence of Nigeria on June 12, 1993. He resides in an exceptionally lovely manor in his home territory of Niger.

During General Ibrahim Babangida's residency, debasement turned into a strategy of the state.[38] He regularly dispensed vehicles and monetary rewards to individuals to procure dependability, and the discipline of the tactical power dissolved. The expression "IBB Young men" arose, an important cause for the head of state in the business domain, somebody who will execute grimy arrangements from drug managing cash laundering.

General Ibrahim Babangida utilized different government privatization drives to remunerate companions and cronies, which at last brought about the ongoing class of nouveau riche in Nigeria. From banking to oil and import licenses, IBB utilized these blessings to raise cash for him as well as his family and is viewed as one of the most extravagant ex-leaders of Nigeria evidently with a huge interest in Globacom— one of the biggest telecom administrators in Nigeria, viewed as a front for his empire.

8. AbachaAdministration (Nov 1993 - June 1998)

The death of General Sani Abacha revealed the global nature of graft. French investigations of bribes paid to government officials to ease the award of a gas plant construction in Nigeria revealed the level of official graft in the country. The investigations led to the freezing of accounts containing about $100 million United States dollars.

In 2000, two years after his demise, a Swiss financial commission report prosecuted Swiss banks for neglecting to follow the consistency cycle when they permitted Abacha's loved ones admittance to his records and to store sums totaling $600 million US dollars in them. Around the same time, a sum of more than $1 billion US dollars was tracked down in different records all through Europe.

9. Abdusalami Administration (June 1998 - May 1999)

The public authority of Gen. Abdusalami was short and centred on travelling the country rapidly to a majority rules system. Though, the doubt stays that a seriously colossal measure of abundance was obtained by him and his internal circle in such a brief period, as he lives in a seriously lovely manor of his own neighbouring IBB's that surpasses anything that he could have procured in genuine pay. For sure, the major Halliburton embarrassment ensnared his organization, and this could have supported his richness.

10. Obasanjo Administration (May 1999 - May 2007)

Different corruption embarrassments broke out under Olusegun Obasanjo's administration, including one of the worldwide aspects when his VP was trapped thick as thieves with a US Representative reserving real money (in a real sense) in coolers. Moreover, the KBR and Siemens pay-off embarrassments broke out under his organization, which was explored by the FBI and prompted global arraignments showing an undeniable level of corruption in his organization. As per reports, "while Nigeria vacillated, the US Branch of Equity on January 18, 2012, declared that a Japanese development firm, Marubeni Company, consented to suffer a $54.6 million criminal consequence for purportedly paying off authorities of the Nigerian government to work with the honour of the $6 billion condensed gaseous petrol contract in Bonny, Nigeria to a global consortium, TSKJ". They offered incentives to Nigerian government authorities somewhere in the range of 1995 and 2004. Obasanjo likewise needed to sack his work serve Hussaini Akwanga on charges that he accepted hush money to endorse a significant government agreement to the French hardware bunch. Obasanjo likewise fired and gave over the Investigator General of Police Mr Tafa Balogun to the EFCC on grounds of debasement to the tune of 5.7 billion. Obasanjo had the option to expand his anti-corruption watchdog by capturing a portion of his ministers that were trapped in payoff and corruption outrages.

Other demonstrations of debasement attached to Olusegun Obasanjo incorporated the Transcorp shares outrage that disregarded the set of rules and norms for public officials and the official library gifts just before his exit from the power that compelled partners to give. Obasanjo was likewise said to generally campaign for his bombed mission to change the constitution to get a third term by effectively paying off the lawmakers; further extending defilement at the most significant levels.

Generally, energy improvement of non-renewables was "up front on the country's plan during its 33 years of military rule, particularly through rebuilding and making new energy enterprises and companies" When Obasanjo got to work in 1999, his administration procured a sensitive state as well as an impractical economy vigorously subject to oil and imbalanced worldwide economic accords. Also, the energy emergency, which was acquired, went on because of the restricted energy area, general legislative shortcomings, and corruption.

11. Umaru Musa Yar'Adua Administration (May 2007 - May 2010)

Yaradua's climb and time in office were short, albeit a fair number of defilement outrages from past organizations became known under his residency and went uninvestigated because of the absence of political will and chronic frailty. Yaradua's different demonstrations of political debasement utilizing his head legal officer to baffle continuous neighbourhood and global examinations of his strong companions like Lead representatives James Ibori, Fortunate Igbinnedion, and Peter Odili which prompted colossal misfortunes to their states. The head legal officer of the League, Michael Aondakaa couldn't get a conviction in that frame of mind as the UK and unfamiliar courts effectively attempted Nigeria's profoundly bad lead representatives from the Obasanjo period that assisted Yaradua with arising as president. What's more, Wikileaks uncovered that the High Court Judges were paid off to legitimize the bad races that saw to his rise as president through far and wide gear. Wikileaks archives likewise uncovered the fortitude of debasement under Yaradua, with unlawful instalments from NNPC to presidents proceeding unabated.

12. Goodluck Jonathan Administration (2010-2015)

Nigeria's defilement rating by TI improved from 143rd to 136th situation in 2014. In late 2013, Nigeria's then National Bank lead representative Sanusi Lamido Sanusi informed President Goodluck Jonathan that the state oil organization, NNPC, had neglected to transmit US$20 billion in oil incomes owed to the state. Jonathan, be that as it may, excused the case and substituted Sanusi for his bungle of the national bank's spending plan. A Senate council likewise observed Sanusi's record to be deficient in substance. After the finish of the NNPC's record review, it was declared in January 2015 that NNPC's non-transmitted income is US$1.48 billion, which it needs to discount to the government. Upon the arrival of the Deloitte report by the public authority just before its leave, it was anyway resolved that really near $20 billion was to be sure absent or misusd or spent without appropriation.

Furthermore, the public authority of Goodluck Jonathan had a few running embarrassments including the BMW bought by his Flight Pastor, to the tune of N255 million Nairaand security agreements with aggressors in the Niger Delta, extensive defilement and payoffs in the Service of Oil, the Malabu Oil Worldwide outrage, and a few outrages including the Petrol Ministry. In the perishing long periods of Goodluck Jonathan's administration, the National Bank outrage of money stumbling of disfigured notes likewise broke out, where it was uncovered that in four days, 8 billion Naira was taken straight by low-level specialists in the CBN. This disclosure prohibited wrongdoing that is thought to have happened for quite a long time and went undetected until uncovered by an informant. The National Bank asserts the heist sabotaged its money-related policy. In 2014, UNODC started a drive to assist with combating defilement in Nigeria.

New charges of corruption have started to arise since the flight of President Jonathan on May 29, 2015, including:

1. $2.2 billion was unlawfully removed from Abundance Unrefined petroleum Accounts,[68] of which $1 billion was endorsed by President Jonathan to support his re-appointment crusade without the information on the Public Financial Chamber comprised of state lead representatives and the president and bad habit president.

2. NEITI found that $11.6 billion was absent from Nigeria LNG Organization profit payments.

3. 60 million barrels of oil esteemed at $13.7 billion were taken under the watch of the public oil organization, Nigerian Public Petrol Company, from 2009 to 2012.

4. NEITI demonstrates misfortunes because of unrefined trades because of endowment and homegrown rough allotment from 2005 to 2012 showed that $11.63 billion

had been paid to the NNPC however that "no proof of the cash is being dispatched to the alliance account".

5. Redirection of 60% of $1 billion in unfamiliar advances acquired from the Chinese by the Ministry of Finance.

6. Gigantic trick in weapons and protection acquisitions, and abuse of 3 trillion naira guard financial plan beginning around 2011 under the guise of fighting Boko Haram.

7. Redirection of $2.2 million immunization medication store, by the Service of Wellbeing

8. Redirection of Ebola fights fund raking 1.9billion Naira.

9. NIMASA misrepresentation being scrutinized by EFCC, comprehensive of an allegation of subsidizing PDP and purchasing a little real estate parcel for 13billion Naira.

10. Service of Money drove by Okonjo Iweala rushed an instalment of $2.2 million to wellbeing service project worker in questioned solicitations.

11. NDDC tricks and diverse tricks including 2.7 billion naira worth of agreements that don't adjust to the Public Acquirement Act.

12. Police Administration Commission Trick researched by ICPC uncovered misappropriation of the north of 150million Naira connected with a political decision related preparing. ICPC made discount suggestions, yet numerous examiners demonstrated arraignment was more appropriate.

13. Muhammadu Buhari Administration (2015-Present)

The administration of Muhammadu Buhari has seen significant activity against debasement in Nigeria. In 2016, the Senate impromptu panel on "mounting philanthropic emergency in the North East" drove by Congressperson Shehu Sani prosecuted the then secretary to the Public authority of the League named Muhammadu Buhari, Mr Babachir Lawal in a N200 million agreement outrage for the getting free from "obtrusive plant species" in Yobe State by Rholavision Nigeria Restricted; an organization he owns.

On October 30, 2017, President Buhari sacked Lawal based on the report of a three-man panel led by Vice-President Yemi Osinbajo that investigated him and one other.

In 2016, Buhari allegedly introduced proof that his head of staff, Abba Kyari, took a N500 million naira pay off from MTN to assist it with slicing the $5 Billion fine banged against it for infringement of Nigeria's broadcast communications guidelines irritating on public security. MTN terminated the staff associated with the payoff scandal. Yet Abba Kyari was left in one piece in his situation as head of staff to public shock constraining Buhari to declare the test of Kyari. The discoveries of the examination were rarely disclosed.

Abdulrasheed Maina was at the top of the team on annuity changes during the President Goodluck Jonathan-drove organization however escaped Nigeria in 2015 after claims that he stole 2billion Naira ($5.6 million, 4.8 million Euros). Albeit an Interpol capture warrant was given, he figured out how to get back to Nigeria, where he was said to have delighted in security from the Buhari government. Maina had been terminated from his situation by Goodluck Jonathan's organization and was put being scrutinized for degenerate practices yet was restored and given a twofold advancement by the Buhari organization.

As indicated by the senate through its board on open records, 85 government parastatals under the current government under the administration of Muhammadu

Buhari are yet to present their review reports starting from the origin of this administration.

The banner conveyor of the defilement battle in Nigeria, the EFCC has answered the senate board of trustees on the public record's case on the non submission of her record report by the organization and 84 others. The Monetary and monetary violations commission denied the report given by the board of trustees guaranteeing it was false.

Despite analysis, the Nigerian Monetary and Monetary Wrongdoings Commission (EFCC) declared in May 2018, that 603 Nigerian figures had been sentenced on defilement allegations since Buhari got to work in 2015. The EFCC likewise declared that without precedent for Nigeria's set of experiences, judges and top military officials including resigned administration bosses are being arraigned for defilement. In December 2019, the country's dubious ex-Principal legal officer Mohammed Adoke, who was blamed for being paid off to concede oil licenses to Shell, was removed to Nigeria from Dubai and was quickly captured. In January 2020, be that as it may, Straightforwardness Global's Defilement Discernment Record (CPI) provided Nigeria with a low positioning of 146 out of 180 nations overviewed.

By October 2020, in any case, End SARS protestors affirmed that Nigerian cops, despite being utilized by what has for some time been seen similar to the worst foundation in Nigeria, were not generally paid satisfactorily and, regardless of getting down on police ruthlessness, required an expansion in police compensations as one of their five requests.

B. Public Establishments Perceived as Corrupt

The accompanying rundown contains the establishments saw as the most corrupt. It is separated from the Nigeria Overview and Corruption Review Study, Last Report (June 2003) Istitute for Development Research, Ahmadu Bello College, Zaria (IDR, ABU Zaria).

Rating Institution

1   Nigerian Police

2   Political Parties

3   National and State Assemblies

4   Local and Municipal Governments

5   Federal and State Executive Councils

6   Traffic Police and Federal Road Safety Corps

7   National Electric Power Authority (NEPA)

In February 2019, it was accounted for that Nigerian Police Power officials normally acquired additional cash by coercing occupants the amount of 50 Nigerian Naira. On July 30, 2019, three Nigeria Police Power Officials from Anambra State were captured on charges of blackmailing three inhabitants. On Walk 9, 2020, two Nigeria Police Power officials from Lagos, Collaborator Director of Police (ASP) Adebayo Ojo and Sergeant Adeleke Mojisola were both captured on charges of blackmailing a lady. The following day, another Nigeria Police Power official from Lagos, Examiner Taloju Martins, was captured subsequent to being discovered on camera blackmailing a driver.

C. Godfatherism

In Nigeria, there is an exceptionally enormous hole between the rich and poor people. Because of this, there is space in legislative issues for more extravagant individuals to control results and competitors. The BBC did an article in February 2019 specifying the amount of an impact 'back up parents' can have on the result. For instance, it was accounted for, "They are political backers, who use cash and impact to win support for their favored up-and-comers." It is made sense of that these 'guardians' groom a competitor that they trust can execute the strategies they need".

CHAPTER 5

Poverty

Nigeria is a country which produces columbite, tantalum, gold, zirconium, tungsten, uranium, thorium and the sky is the limit from there. As far as creation of columbite, Nigeria is a world chief, and it enters the best ten with regards to tin mining. Regardless of the way that the nation is so wealthy in regular assets, individuals of Nigeria live beneath the neediness line. Many individuals in the nation can't take care of themselves appropriately. 20% of Nigerian populace scarcely earn enough to get by, and just around 10% are agreeable. The distinction among rich and poor in this nation arrives at a level unbelievable. In the capital of Nigeria you can track down the most sumptuous estates and vehicles.

What causes neediness in Nigeria? There are many explanations behind neediness, and they are different in each country. Talking about reasons for outright destitution in Nigeria, we determined the accompanying ones:

1. Government Corruption

Since its foundation, government corruption overran Nigeria. This is one of the significant purposes behind destitution in the country. Government specialists consistently take installments from oil organizations that ought to go into public trusts - installments which can frequently be more than USD 1 billion - and rather siphon that money into their ledgers.

At the point when government specialists participate in these defilement plots, poor people and the under-served in Nigeria are most certainly impacted. Assuming these colossal measures of cash quit going into government specialists' records, that cash could be utilized for the improvement of the nation's foundation - roads, running water from there, the sky is the limit.

2. Absence of Monetary Framework

Foundation is vital for the country for some reasons, and it assumes a huge part with regards to rising up out of destitution. Monetary framework in Nigeria includes admittance to miniature advances that assist ranchers with keeping their homestead and make their residing.

One more reason for poverty is the way that most Nigerians are basically gridlocked under particular conditions and they don't do not have the ability to change something in their lives. With a stable financial framework, which would offer Nigerians the chance to create, the flourishing of the nation will happen quickly.

3. Poor Access to Education

One of the reasons for poverty in Nigeria is poor/unfortunate admittance to education. Schooling is the establishment that allows an individual an opportunity to have a fruitful profession in future. Be that as it may, tragically, not every person approaches this fundamental establishment. Right now, the least fortunate individuals in Nigeria essentially have no steady admittance to education/training. 10.5 million Nigerian kids don't go to class by any means, and 60% of these youngsters are young ladies.

These issues are most normal in the Northern part of the country. Likewise, Boko Haram fear mongers, who secured themselves as the impassioned adversaries of Western instruction, stoke the fire. Schooling gives the apparatuses expected to the work and expert turn of events, and absence of these open doors is one of the harming reasons for poverty in Nigeria.

4. Poor Accessto Medical Services

Nigeria is perhaps of the biggest country in Africa concerning populace, yet the nature of clinical benefits in the nation falls excessively far behind. Also, obviously, unfortunate/poor access to medical care is one more reason for poverty.

Because of an absence of subject matter experts and meds, many individuals in Nigeria either are not treated by any means, or they don't get legitimate clinical benefits. Furthermore, therapy is frequently costly, and that is another justification for why individuals don't get clinical consideration. Further developing admittance to Nigerian medical services is a significant stage to decrease poverty in Nigeria. From the outset, this large number of issues can appear to be confounded and practically unsolvable. However, understanding the issue and knowing the beginning of its root is critical to tracking down the arrangement. UNICEF and the UN have sent off a few drives to fortify the economy, schooling and to further develop medical services in Nigeria and lessen the degree of defilement among the specialists. Thus, Nigeria shows its capacity to help out unfamiliar accomplices and the longing to work on the existence of individuals. Trying sincerely and finding viable answers for issues is the exit from poverty.

THE World Bank has said that the rising costs of food things in the nation could drive extra 6,000,000 Nigerians into poverty.

The World Bank in a distribution with the title, Coronavirus in Nigeria: Frontline Data and Pathways for Policy, said, "The rise in costs saw between June 2020 and June 2021 alone could drive one more 6 million Nigerians into poverty/neediness, with metropolitan regions being lopsidedly impacted."

The National Bureau of Statistics (NBS) had, on Monday, said that the yearly food expansion rate increased for the 24th sequential month to 20.75 percent in October from 20.71 percent in September because of additional expansions in the costs of fundamental food things.

In itsConsumer Price Index, CPI and Expansion Report for October 2021, that's what NBS noticed "This ascent in the food file was brought about by expansions in costs of food items, espresso, tea and cocoa, milk, cheddar and eggs, bread and cereals, vegetables and potatoes, sweet potato and different tubers." Thus, food expansion rate had increased by 7.38 rate focuses since May 2019 when it dropped to 13.37 percent.

The World Bank included the report, "The portion of Nigerians living beneath the national poverty line might have expanded from 40.1 percent to 42.8 percent, because of the food cost expansion saw between June 2020 and June 2021. This implies around 5.6 million extra Nigerians would be living in neediness.

While food value expansion would diminish buying power and raise poverty across Nigeria, apparently metropolitan regions could be excessively impacted.

As per the worldwide body, while the initial segment of the Coronavirus emergency encouraged a worldwide financial log jam which caused a downturn in Nigeria, the subsequent emergency was described by flooding expansion, coming down on families' buying power.

The bank expressed, "In April 2021, the year-on-year expansion rate was the most noteworthy in four years, and food costs represented more than 60% of the absolute increase in inflation.

"Without a doubt, in 2020 and 2021, Nigeria saw its most noteworthy flood in food-cost inflation in very nearly twenty years. This inflationary tension stems from both organic market factors, a significant number of which are straightforwardly connected to the Coronavirus emergency.

CHAPTER 6

Unemployment

The President of the African Development Bank, AfDB, Akinwumi Adesina, has deplored the high pace of joblessness among Nigerians, saying regarding 40% of young people were unemployed.

Adesina, who revealed this at a talk in Lagos, said the young people were deterred, irate and fretful, as they take a gander at a future that doesn't give them trust.

Joblessness among youthful Nigerians (15-34 years) is the most elevated in the country, with 21.72 million or 42.5 percent of the 29.94 youthful Nigerians in the workforce jobless, while the public unemployment rate remained at 33.3 percent as of December 2020.

Any graduate after school hopes to get a well-paying position after the finish of his examinations, yet the truth in Nigeria's work area has demonstrated in any case as there is no significant work anywhere after the obligatory National Youth Service Corps (NYSC) program. Be that as it may, back in the mid 70s, the activity varied as new college and polytechnic graduates, even alumni of educators' schools, had occupations sitting tight for them going from administrative to proficient positions in light of their areas of specialization.

Albeit the nation had this sort of arrangement of government before then, at that point, what changed the destiny of the Nigerian alumni and how can it connect up to the current issues and difficulties looked by the public authority, particularly in the space of frailty?

Unemployment is what is going on by which people fit and able to work can't track down appropriate paid job. Joblessness is one of the serious issues in Nigeria since it has caused such countless issues like uncertainty, banditry, abducting and other related acts.

The arrangement of the nation has separated; as no area is well-playing out that can retain or diminish the pace of joblessness and this outcomes in an elevated degree of neediness which makes such countless young people take part in crimes.

There are other causative elements for the high joblessness rate in Nigeria, which has been representing a major danger to the tremendous populace. One of these is corruption, another challenge, as preference and nepotism became key necessities for work position and substitution in both the private and public areas. Today occupations are not being given in light of legitimacy and these have denied capable Nigerians the potential chance to be utilized in any area in the country.

Notwithstanding, there is a platitude that each infection has its fix; similarly, every issue has its answer. Luckily, this joblessness circumstance in Nigeria isn't without an answer, one of which is that the public authority ought to invest more energy into battling corruption at all levels, both in the private and public areas.

Likewise, there is a need to broaden the economy from the oil area to give greater need to different method for producing pay as this will decrease the pace of joblessness such countless young people will profit from the activity. Nearby business people ought to likewise be given thought; while the public authority ought to establish an empowering climate for Small and Medium-scale Enterrprises (SMEs), to make due and develop.

How Is UnemploymentEstimated?

Joblessness is when individuals are prepared, capable and able to work, however do not find work. By the Worldwide Work Association definition, an individual is utilized when they work something like 40 hours per week. The working-age is viewed as somewhere in the range of 15 and 60. Presently, 33.3% or 23.2 million of the around 70 million individuals who ought to be working in Nigeria are jobless. A satisfactory degree of joblessness would be 4%-6%.

The country's underemployment rate - individuals who work under 20 hours per week - is likewise high at 22.8%.

What's Driving Joblessness In Nigeria?

One component is the basically unfortunate condition of the economy. The economy has not been looking great for the past five years and first went into a downturn in 2016.

In 2020 directly following the Coronavirus pandemic, it dove into another downturn - its most awful in forty years. It recorded a GDP constriction of 3.62% in the second from last quarter of 2020.

There's been a ton of vulnerability, generally because of strategy irregularities, about where individuals ought to contribute. This cuts across different financial areas.

Since the ongoing government came into power in 2015, there has been a ton of strategy change with the "order and control" act took on in dealing with the economy. For example, trade rates were left fixed for the principal year of the organization until the contortions in the market became turbulent before some type of adaptability was permitted in the assurance of the swapping scale, following market influences. Likewise, land borders were randomly shut to imports, notwithstanding the gigantic harm it could include on the nation's exchange inside the ECOWAS sub-district. This straightforwardly affected the costs of things.

These strategy somersaults have caused capital flight. The political vulnerability assumed a part in the descending pattern of business sectors. In the values market, enormous unfamiliar portfolio ventures were lost to the economy. There has likewise been a slump in portfolio ventures, fixed capital speculation, unfamiliar direct ventures and capital importation. There was likewise a record decrease in capital importation of about $1,548.88 million in the final quarter of 2016, a 15% diminishing from the second from last quarter of that very year.

Also, in the main quarter of 2017, capital importation was recorded to be about $908.27 million.

The outcome has been employment misfortunes and the decreasing ability to make occupations.

The poor performance of various areas of the economy, particularly the horticultural area, has made vulnerability and joblessness. The repetitive rancher herder emergency has hurt agrarian work and creation.

Another issue is Nigeria's powerless/weak currency, which has been terrible for assembling and manufacturing. As many individuals just approach unfamiliar cash through informal sources, costs of unrefined substances for assembling have impacted the area and its result. A few associations can't scale or employ more individuals.

The low degree of framework in the economy is another basic element. For example, ranchers need to move their products to business sectors. The courses that connect the ranches to the urban communities are in unfortunate shape. The power supply is unpredictable and security is poor. These elements amount to an unfortunate degree of input.

In the interim, the work supply is developing. Individuals are moving on from higher organizations, however the interest for work is contracting. There are insufficient positions for youngsters who are leaving school. Individuals with A levels as their most noteworthy capability had the most noteworthy pace of joblessness with 50.7%, trailed by individuals with a first degree or higher public recognition at 40.1%.

How Much More Terrible Has Coronavirus Made Things?

Measures like lockdowns, social separating, telecommute and travel limitations fundamentally impacted the economy. The avionics area and related administrations were perhaps of the most awful hit. The diversion area - motion pictures, sports, shows - was trapped in the stay at home order. The little and medium-scale industry was likewise gravely hit, especially miniature organizations - the individuals who procure on an everyday premise.

Indeed, even with the opening up of the economy, the impacts remain. Furthermore, we don't know Coronavirus is disappearing in a rush.

CONCLUSION

The way forward

Nigeria with its rich mineral resources remains one of the poorest nations in the world. Minute per cent of the entire populace is rich while a vast per cent is extremely poor.

Insecurity, unemployment, poverty, corruption and poor education are still ravaging the country to date. The nation is wailing, children are crying, hungry and walking aimlessly on the street with a bleak ray of hope for a better tomorrow and inflation catapulting to its peak to a point where the citizens can merely afford three square meals. There is a call for an urgent need to curb these hurricanes by the government.

Without this approach, the migration of our youths in search of greener pastures to the western world will be on the high rise as they will view it as the only way to a better tomorrow.